About the Author

Mr. Paul Watson has many years of experience in Continuous Integration with TeamCity. He has worked on large software projects in USA, UK, Singapore, Hong Kong, Dubai, Australia and Switzerland.

His hobbies include travelling to new tourist places, watching basketball, cricket, Soccer and learning latest technological stuff.

Preface

This book is for those who are new to Team City. It will help you understand what is TeamCity and how you can use it in your software project.

Below topics are covered in this book.

Welcome to the TeamCity tutorial. In this tutorial, you will learn below topics.

1. Introduction
2. Installing trail version of TeamCity
3. User and groups in TeamCity
4. Projects in TeamCity
5. Project configurations
6. Build Configurations
7. Build steps
8. Build actions
9. Build agents in TeamCity
10. Tracking changes
11. Managing Build Queue
12. Personalizing TeamCity
13. More administration

1. Introduction

TeamCity is the most popular Continuous Integration server in the world. It was developed by the company JetBrains (http://www.jetbrains.com/teamcity/)

Features of Team city

1. Allows multiple build agents
2. Runs on Amazon Cloud
3. Allows multiple build configuration and build steps
4. Multiple users with different rights can be created through web interface
5. Provides dashboard for viewing reports
6. Gated commits - allows remote testing before committing and pushing
7. We can view who changed what in vcs
8. Integration with popular IDEs like Visual Studio, Intellij IDEA
9. works with all popular version control systems (VCS) GIT, SVN, Team foundation server

2. Installing trail version of TeamCity

TeamCity server is built on the top of tomcat server.

You can Grab your trial copy of team city on below link

http://www.jetbrains.com/teamcity/

Below images show how to install TeamCity on windows.

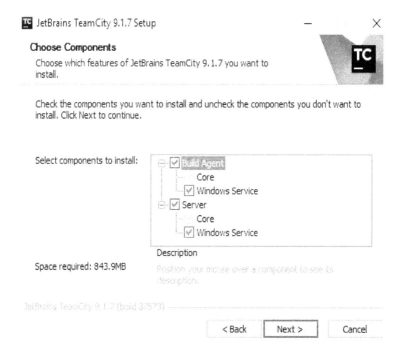

Database connection setup

Select the database type: Internal (HSQLDB) ▼

The internal database suits evaluation purposes only and is no

You can start with the internal database and then migrate the d

Proceed

TC JetBrains TeamCity 9.1.7 Setup — ✕

Select Service Account for Server

TC

Specify a user account to run TeamCity Server service:

○ Run TeamCity Server under the SYSTEM account
◉ Run TeamCity Server under a user account

< Back | Next > | Cancel

Notice that I have changed the TeamCity port from 8080 to 8888.

Configure Build Agent Properties — □ X

Build Agent Properties

Property	Value
serverUrl	http://localhost:8888
name	Sagar-Windows10
ownPort	9090
systemDir	C:\TeamCity\buildAgent\system
workDir	C:\TeamCity\buildAgent\work
tempDir	C:\TeamCity\buildAgent\temp
env.TEAMCITY_JRE	C:\Program Files\Java\jdk1.7.0_79

Add

Edit

Remove

env.TEAMCITY_JRE	value should be the JDK home directory (in case you want to run Java builds).
name	value is the name of an agent that will be displayed in the TeamCity user interface.
ownPort	value is a port where the agent listens to the server commands. Please make sure this port is not blocked by firewall.
serverUrl	value is the TeamCity server location.
workDir	value is the working catalogue where the builds are being built.
tempDir	value is the temp catalogue being used by agent.

* The Build Agent properties file is stored in the 'conf' directory of the Build Agent installation folder where you can edit it later.

Save   Close

You can start the TeamCity server by using below command.

C:\TeamCity\bin\startup.bat

 ## TeamCity First Start

Please review the settings below before proceeding with the first TeamCity start

TeamCity server stores configuration settings on disk in a **Data Directory**.

Location of the Data Directory: C:\Users\Sagar\.BuildServer

If you already worked with TeamCity on this machine or want to use another directory.

Proceed

 ## TeamCity is starting

Initializing TeamCity server components

Create Administrator Account

Version 9.1.7 (build 37573)

* Username: sagar
* Password: ....
* Once again: ....|

Create Account

Once installed, you can access the TeamCity web interface through popular browser.

3. Users and groups in TeamCity

3.1 User management in TeamCity

Now let us see how to manage users in TeamCity. We can manage users from Admin page as shown in below images.

To add new user, click on Create user account. Then new form will appear as shown in second image.

Users in TeamCity

Just fill all information like username, password, email. You can also make new user an administrator if you want.

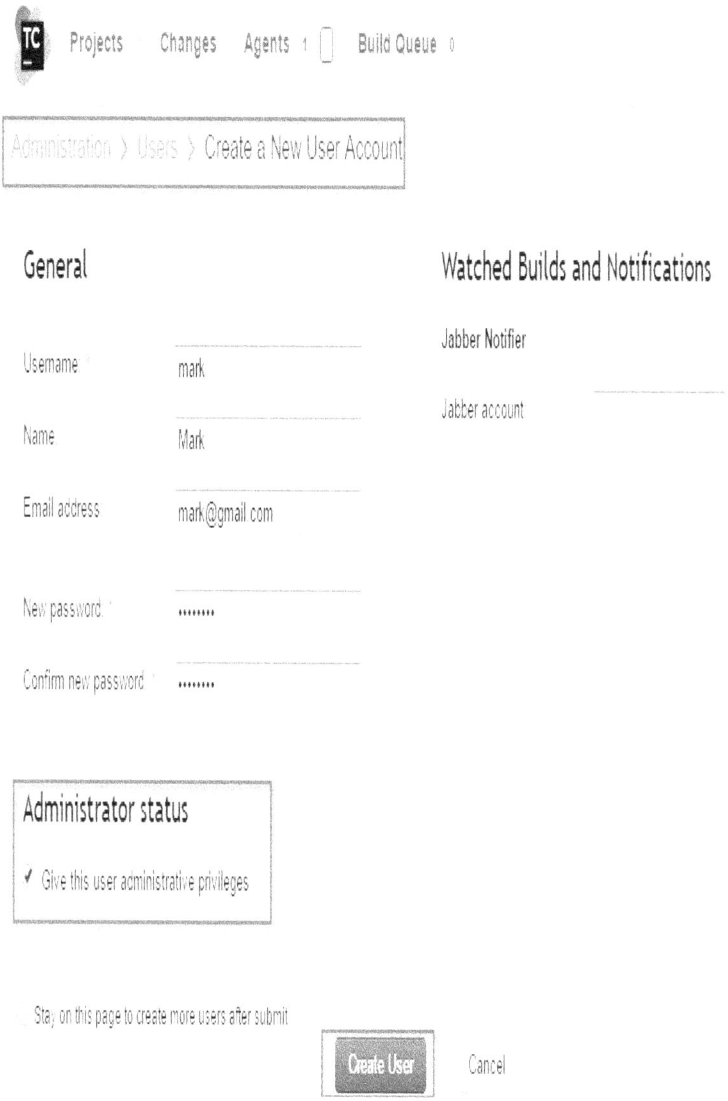

Adding new user in TeamCity

To remove user from TeamCity, just select the check box in front of the user and click on remove button as shown in below image.

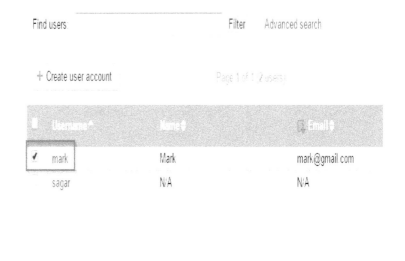

Removing users in TeamCity

3.2 Group management in TeamCity

Now let us see how to manage the groups in TeamCity. You can access Group settings in Administration page. To create new group, just click on Create new group button as shown in below image.

As shown in below image, you have to enter group name and key.

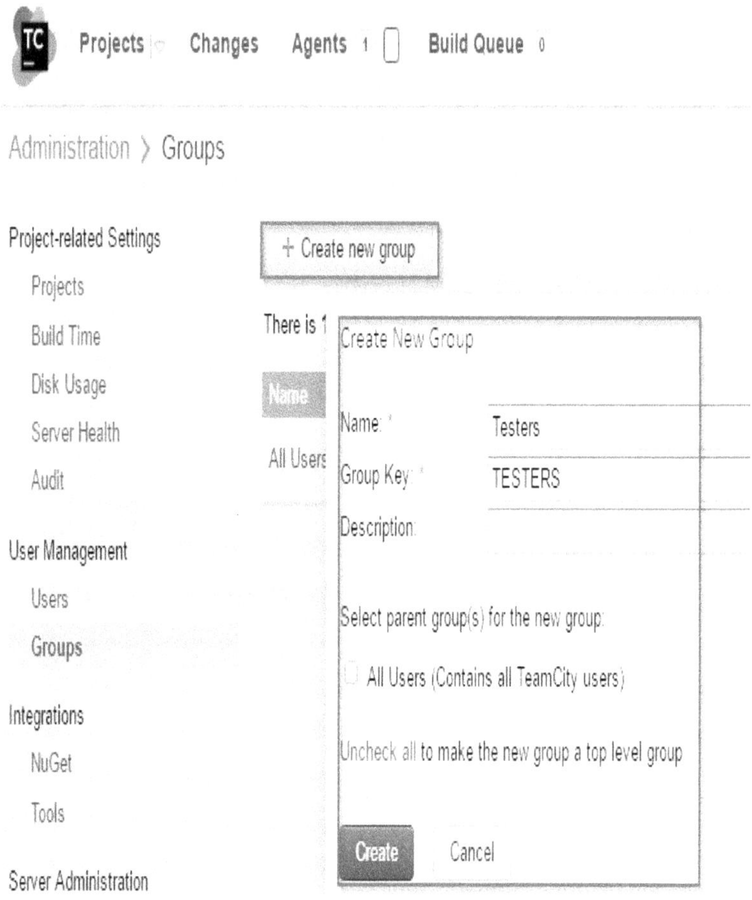

4. Projects in TeamCity

4.1 Setting up the projects

We can have multiple projects in team city. Each project can have multiple builds.

We can create a project from scratch or by using source code url as shown in below image.

New project in TeamCity

Each project has below settings.

1. General - Name, project id, description, build configuration and templates, sub-projects
2. VCS roots - Here we specify the repository of project source
3. Builds Schedule - here we can configure the schedules for the build
4. SSH Keys - The settings is used to specify the SSH keys used for VCS authentication purposes.
5. Clean up rules - Here we can set up rules to perform clean up tasks like backing up the build output etc.
6. Version settings

4.2 Creating project from scratch

You can create a new TeamCity project from Administration tab provided that you have enough permission to create a new project.

Maven Project in TeamCity

Create new maven build configuration in TeamCity

TC Projects   Changes   Agents 1 ☐   Build Queue 0

Administration 〉 ▫ <Root project> 〉 ▫ Maven Project 〉 Create Build Configuration

Name: Maven tests

Build configuration ID: MavenProject_MavenTests

This ID is used in URLs, REST API, HTTP requests to the server and configuration

Description: |

Create   Cancel

Maven test build in TeamCity

VCS settings for a build in TeamCity

Build configuration successfully created. You can now configure VCS roots.

Type of VCS

Type of VCS: Git

VCS Root

VCS root name: maventestnggit

A unique name to distinguish this VCS root from other roots

VCS root ID: MavenProject_Maventestnggit

VCS root ID must be unique across all VCS roots. VCS root ID can be used in parameter references to VCS root parameters and REST API.

General Settings

Fetch URL: https://github.com/reply2sagar/TestNG-Project.git

This is used for fetching data from the repository.

Push URL:

It is used for pushing tags to the remote repository. If blank, the fetch url is used.

Default branch: refs/heads/master

The main branch to be monitored.

Authentication Settings

New Build Step

Runner type:	Maven ▾
	Runs Maven builds
Step name:	test
	Optional: specify to distinguish this build step from other steps
Goals:	test
	Space-separated goals to execute.
Path to POM file:	pom.xml
	The specified path should be relative to the checkout directory

Code Coverage

Choose coverage runner: <No coverage> ▾

Show advanced options

Save   Cancel

maven test goal in Team City

4.3 Creating project by URL

You can create a project from source code repository url (like git repository). Below image will show how I created gradle project from url.

First of all, you need to provide the url of git repository.

Creating gradle project from URL

Then you need to provide project name and build configuration name.

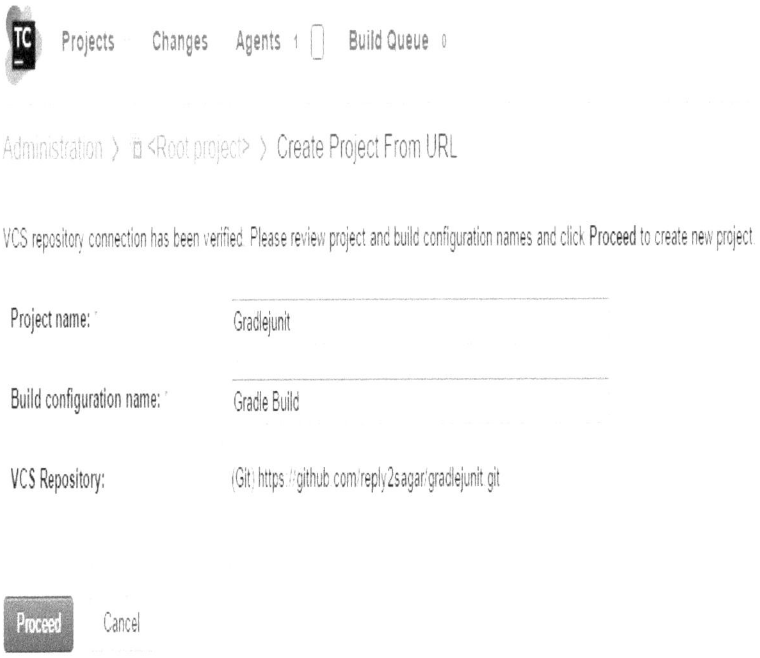

New build project name TeamCity

TeamCity detects the build steps by looking at the source code. As shown in below image, TeamCity has detected 3 build steps - command line, Gradle and IntelliJ IDEA project. Out of those, I selected Gradle step.

Auto detected build steps in TeamCity

Next you can run the build by clicking on run button.

TC   Projects   Changes   Agents 1 ☐   Build Queue 0   sagar

Administration ⟩ ☐ <Root project> ⟩ ☐ Gradlejunit ⟩ ☐ Gradle Build   ⟳ Run

☐ Build Configuration Settings

General Settings

Version Control Settings 1

Build Step: Gradle

Triggers

Failure Conditions

Build Features

Dependencies

Parameters

Agent Requirements

Last edited **6 minutes ago** by **sagar** (view history)

Name: Gradle Build

Build configuration ID: Gradlejunit_GradleBuild
This ID is used in URLs, REST API, HTTP request in the TeamCity Data Directory

Description:

Artifact paths:

Newline-separated paths of files or directories to wildcards like dir/**/*.zip and target directorie a target directory are supported. The paths can a

🔧 Show advanced options

Save   Cancel

Run the build in TeamCity

Below image shows how the TeamCity build looks like when it is running.

Gradle build running in TeamCity

4.4 Viewing all projects, sub-projects and builds in TeamCity

To view all projects, sub-projects and build configurations in each of them, you have to go to administration page. Then click on the Projects link in the left navigation bar.

Viewing all projects, sub-projects and builds in TeamCity

From projects page, you can do below things.

1. Create new project
2. Create new project from url
3. You can filter the projects
4. Edit projects and sub-projects
5. Edit builds
6. Copy, move, archive, delete the project
7. Copy, move, delete the build configuration
8. Please see below screenshots for more details.

copy, move, delete project in TeamCity

copy, move, delete build configuration in TeamCity

4.5 Project page in TeamCity

When you open any project in TeamCity, you can view below tabs.

1. Project overview - displays all builds, if build has pending changes, status of last build run, changes in last build run. We can also run and stop the build
2. Change log - shows the changes of the project source code
3. Statistics - Here we can view the project graphs
4. Current problems - shows the problems in the project like build failures
5. Investigations - shows the data about investigations in the project.
6. Muted problems - We can suppress some problems in the builds.
7. Webhooks

Accessing project page in TeamCity

tabs on project page in TeamCity

4. 6 Configuring visible projects

By default, TeamCity shows all projects on Projects Page (Dashboard). But you may not be interested in all projects. We can make only specific projects visible on the dashboard by configuring visible projects in TeamCity as shown in below image.

In below image, we have hidden project - Vstestrepo. Only 2 projects will be shown on dashboard - Maven Project and Gradlejunit

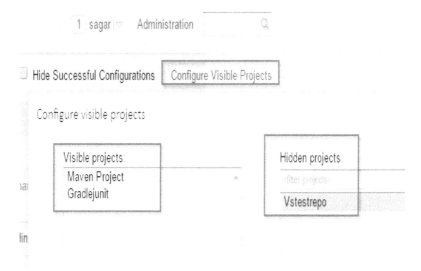

Configuring visible projects in TeamCity

5. Project configurations

Every project in TeamCity has below settings.

1. General settings - It contains project name, project Id, builds. We can also create new build configuration from here. We can also create sub-projects in current project.
2. VCS roots - It contains VCS settings. For example - git url.
3. Report Tabs - Here we can access build artifacts and reports.
4. Parameters - This setting allows us to pass any parameter or variable to the build.
5. Builds Schedule - It shows all build schedules of the project.
6. Issue Trackers
7. SSH Keys - You can store SSH keys for authentication over here.
8. Meta Runners
9. Shared Resources
10. Clean up rules
11. Version Settings

Project configuration in TeamCity

5.1 General settings

On general project settings, we can configure below things.

1. Project name
2. Project Id
3. Project Description
4. Create a build configuration
5. Create build configuration template
6. Create sub-project

Below images show all these settings in TeamCity.

Projects   Changes   Agents 0 [ ]   Build Queue 0

Administration 〉 ⊡ <Root project> 〉 ⊡ Maven Project

⊡ Project Settings

General Settings

VCS Roots   1

Report Tabs

Parameters

Builds Schedule

Issue Trackers

Shared Resources

Meta-Runners

SSH Keys

Maven Settings

Clean-up Rules

Versioned Settings

Created 7 days ago by sagar
(view history)

Name: *

Maven Project

Project ID: *

MavenProject

This ID is used in URLs, REST API, HTTP re

Description:

Save   Cancel

Build Configurations (11 left)

Build configurations define how to retrieve and build sources of a project

　+ Create build configuration　　+ Create build configuration from URL

Name

Code inspection build

CompileMavenBuild

Duplicate finder build

Build Configuration Templates

Build configuration templates define settings that can be reused by different build configurations. ⑦

+ Create template

Name		Build Steps
MavenTemplate	Used in 1 configuration	test

Subprojects

Subprojects can be used to group build configurations and define projects hierarchy within a single project. ⑦

+ Create subproject   + Create subproject from URL

5.2 VCS roots

In this article, let us see how to create VCS roots for a project in TeamCity.

Under project settings, click on VCS roots link. From VCS roots page, we can add new VCS root, edit existing VCS root or delete it.

To create new VCS root, click on **Create VCS root** button.

VCS roots in TeamCity project

On new VCS root page, you can select one of the supported VCS systems.

1. ClearCase
2. CVS
3. Git
4. Mercurial
5. Perforce
6. SubVersion (SVN)
7. Team Foundation Server
8. Visual Source Safe

Administration > <Root project> > Maven Project > New VCS Root

Type of VCS

Type of VCS:

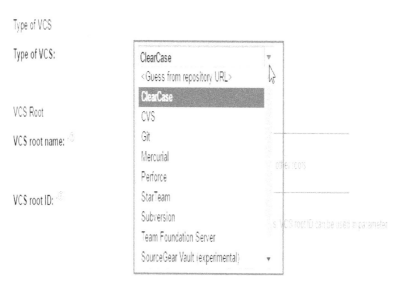

VCS Root

VCS root name:

VCS root ID:

VCS root types in TeamCity

Below image shows how to configure git VCS root.

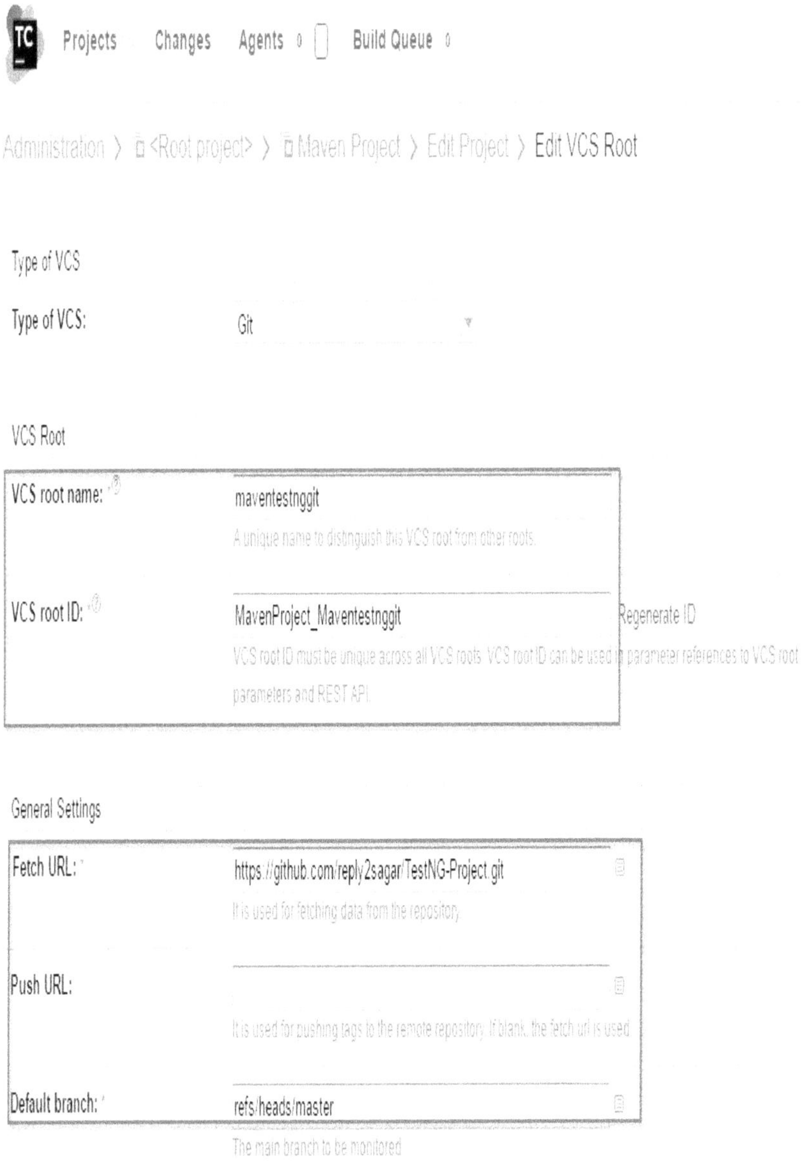

git VCS root in TeamCity

5.3 Creating report tabs for projects and builds

Report tab settings allow you to create custom report tabs that are displayed on Project and Build pages.

For example - In maven project, surefire reports are generated. We can save those reports in artifacts. To view those reports, we can configure report tab for a build or project.

Below image shows how to create a build report tab. Please note that path of the Start page of the report should be relative to the artifacts stored on TeamCity.

Creating report tab in TeamCity

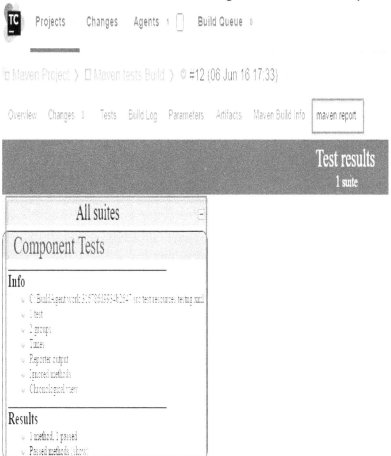

Build page showing report tab in TeamCity

5.4 Build schedules of a Projects

You can view all Builds Schedule of a project as shown in below image.

As you can see, below project has 1 build schedule on 06 June 2016. That build runs daily at 19:00 hrs in Brisbane time zone.

This page shows only enabled schedules. To view disabled and paused build schedules, you need to click on advanced options and then filter the results.

Viewing Builds Schedule of a project in TeamCity

5.6 SSH keys for authentication purpose

We can add SSH keys at a project level in TeamCity as shown in below image. If you want to know how SSH keys work, please watch this video on **SSH keys and GIT** (https://www.youtube.com/watch?v=ZNER9rHjQ2Q)

Uploading SSH keys in TeamCity

5.9 Clean-up rules of a project

Clean up process runs periodically on TeamCity server. Clean-up process helps us optimize the server performance. By default, when the clean up process runs, it deletes artifacts of builds.

But if you want, you can customize the default behavior of clean up process for specific project as shown in below image.

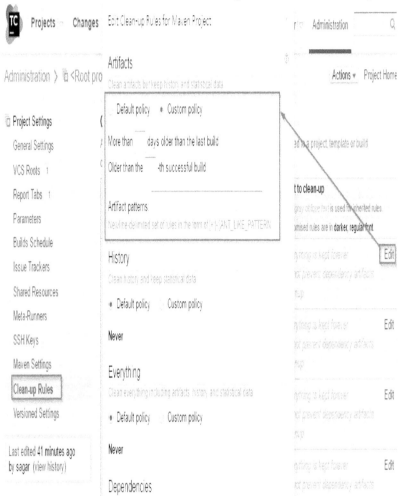

Clean up rules of project in TeamCity

5.10 Project actions

We can take below actions on a project in TeamCity.

1. Copy project
2. Move project to different project
3. Delete a project
4. Archive a project
5. Reorder build configurations
6. Bulk edit ids of a project

Below image shows how to access these actions.

Project actions in TeamCity

6. Build Configurations

Below is the list of build configuration settings, we can make while configuring the build.

1. **General** - Name, ID, Description, Artifact paths, Build number format: %build.counter%, Build options:Enable hanging builds detection, Enable status widget, Limit the number of simultaneously running builds (0 — unlimited): unlimited
2. **VCS settings** - VCS checkout mode: Automatically on server, Checkout directory: default, Clean all files before build: ON, Attached VCS roots - repository url
3. **Build steps** - You can as many build steps as you want in your build. We will see build steps in detail in following sections
4. Triggers - VCS trigger, schedule trigger, Finish build trigger, Branch remote run trigger, Maven artifact dependency trigger, maven snapshot dependencies trigger, Nuget dependency trigger, retry build trigger (We can pause triggers as well as build queue)
5. **Failure conditions** - drives when build run should be marked as failed. (when at least one test fails, runner exit code is non-zero etc)
6. **Build features**
7. **Dependencies** - Snapshot dependencies and artifact dependencies

8. **Parameters** - We can pass the parameters to build before running the test. Configuration parameters and Environment Variables

9. **Build Agent requirements** - We can specify all hardware and software features required on the build agents in this setting

Build configuration settings in TeamCity

6.1 General settings of a build configuration (artifact paths)

Here is the list of general settings of a build configuration in TeamCity.

1. Build name
2. Build Id - Unique Id of the build
3. Description
4. Build number format - Format of each build run number
5. Build counter - Shows current build number. We can reset it.
6. Artifact paths - specify the location of build output files to be stored. This is very important setting. Artifacts can be used to troubleshoot problems occured in build run.
7. Detect if any build is hanging

Below image shows sample general settings of a build in TeamCity

☐ Build Configuration Settings

General Settings

Version Control Settings 1

Build Step: Maven

Triggers

Failure Conditions

Build Features

Dependencies

Parameters

Agent Requirements

Last edited **5 minutes ago**
by **sagar** (view history)

Name: * Maven tests Build

Build configuration ID: * MavenProject_MavenTests   Regenerate ID

This ID is used in URLs, REST API, HTTP requests to the server and configuration settings
in the TeamCity Data Directory.

Description:

Build number format: %build.counter%

The format may include %build.counter% as a placeholder for the build counter value. For
example 1.%build.counter%.
It may also contain a reference to any other available parameter, for example
%build.vcs.number.VCSRootName%.
Note: The maximum length of a build number after all substitutions is 256 characters.

Build counter: * 12   Reset

Artifact paths: /target/surefire-reports/**   Reset

Newline-separated paths of files or directories to publish as build artifacts. Ant-style
wildcards like dir/**/*.zip and target directories like out/*.zip => dist, where dist is
a target directory, are supported. The paths can also be separated by commas.

Build options: ✓ enable hanging builds detection
✓ allow triggering personal builds
☐ enable status widget

Limit the number of simultaneously running builds (0 — unlimited): 0

General settings of build configuration

6.2 Version control settings of a build

In version control settings of a build, we can do below things.

1. Attache VCS root
2. Edit VCS root
3. Detach VCS root
4. Edit checkout rules

Below image shows that we have added git VCS root to the build.

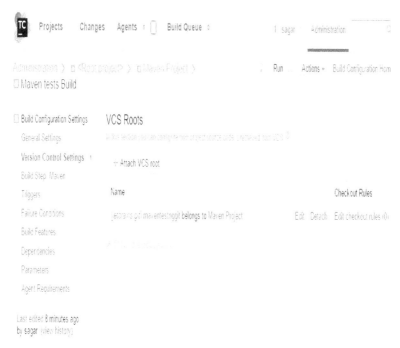

Build configuration - Version control settings in TeamCity

6.3 Build steps

We can add build steps in 2 ways.

1. Manually
2. Automatically - TeamCity detects steps by looking at VCS sources.

Below image shows that we have added a test step to build.

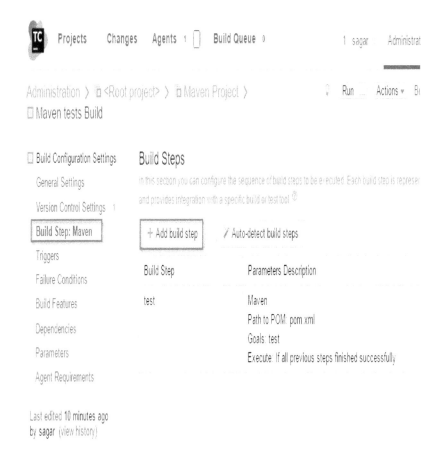

Build step configuration in TeamCity

Various other build steps that can be added are shown in below images.

New Build Step

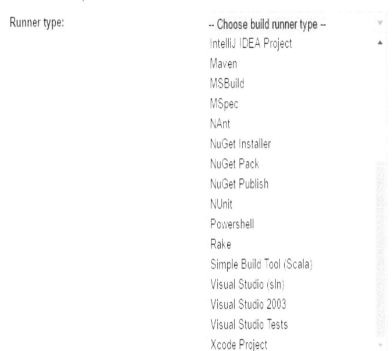

6.4 Adding build triggers

Below image shows what kind of triggers can be used in TeamCity. Some of the popular triggers are -

1. VCS trigger - TeamCity polls VCS periodically and if changes are detected, builds are triggered.
2. Schedule trigger - In this type of trigger, we set up the build to run at specific time of the day.

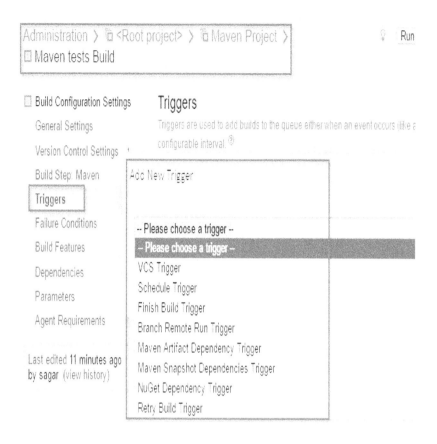

Below image shows sample schedule trigger. We have scheduled the trigger in such a way that builds will be run every Saturday @ 23 Hrs in Australia/Brisbane time zone.

Schedule Trigger

Triggering Conditions   Additional Options

Trigger build if all of the following conditions are met.

Date and Time

| When: | weekly ▼ |

| Day of the week: | Saturday ▼ |

| Time (HH:mm): | 23 ▼ 00 ▼ |

| Timezone: | Server Time Zone - AEST Australia/Brisbane (UTC+10) ▼ |

VCS Changes

☑ Trigger only if there are pending changes

Trigger rules:⑦   Edit Trigger Rules

                    + Add new rule

Build Changes

☐ Trigger only if watched build changes ⑦

6.5 Adding failure conditions for a build

By default, a build fails when either of below things happen.

1. Build process exits with non-zero code
2. at least one test fails
3. Build process crashes

We can edit these settings from failure conditions page as shown in below image.

But TeamCity also allows us to add extra failure conditions. There are 2 broad categories of failure conditions that can be added.

1. Fail when a build log contains specific text
2. Fail when certain metric condition is met. For example - fail when artifact size more than 1 GB or When build duration is more than 20 minutes.

Below images show how we set up these failure conditions for a build.

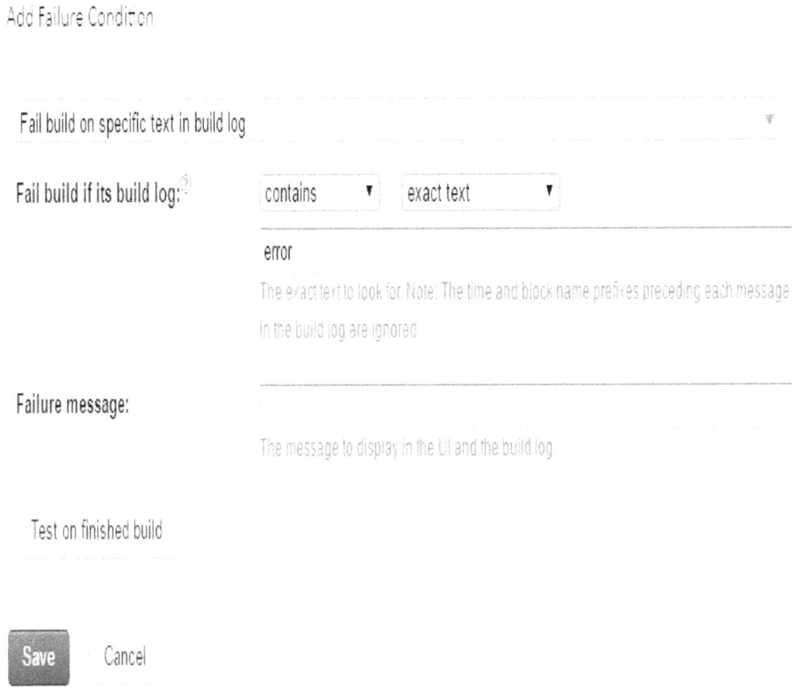

Add Failure Condition

Fail build on specific text in build log

Fail build if its build log: contains   ▾   exact text   ▾

error

The exact text to look for. Note: The time and block name prefixes preceding each message in the build log are ignored.

Failure message:

The message to display in the UI and the build log

Test on finished build

Save   Cancel

Fail build when specific text is found in log in TeamCity

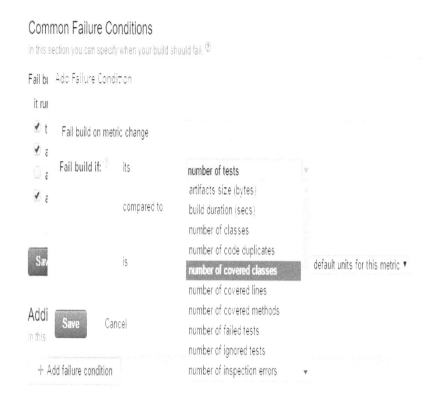

Fail build on metric change in TeamCity

6. 6 Passing parameters to build

We can pass the parameters to build as shown in below image.

We can pass 3 types of parameters to build.

1. Configuration parameters

2. System properties

3. Environment variables

Passing parameter to the build configuration

6.7 Build Configuration actions

We can do below actions on Build configuration in TeamCity.

1. Pause/Resume triggers - This actions allows you to disable or enable any future build triggers.
2. Copy build configuration
3. Move build configuration - This action allows you to move your build configuration from one project to another.
4. Delete build configuration
5. Extract meta-runner
6. Extract build configuration template -This action allows you to create a build configuration template based on existing build configuration.

Below image shows how we can do all these actions.

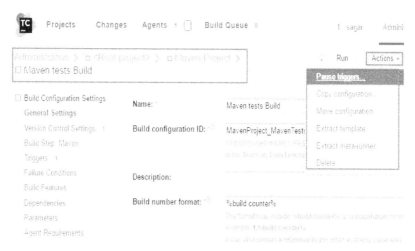

Build configuration actions in TeamCity

6.8 Build configuration templates

In this topic, you will learn how to create Build configuration templates. Main benefit of using templates is that you can create new build configurations very quickly.

You can create Build configuration templates in 2 ways.

1. Manually
2. Extracting template from existing build configuration

To add a template manually, you have to go to the project settings page and then click on create a new build configuration template as shown in below image.

Create build template manually in TeamCity

Below image shows how to create a new Build configuration template by extracting it from existing build configuration.

Extract template from build in TeamCity

Extract Template

Template name: *	gradleTemplate
	Note that this build configuration will be attached to the extracte template.
Template ID: * ⑦	Gradlejunit_GradleTemplate

Extract   Cancel

New template name in TeamCity

Once new template is created, it is displayed under project from where it is extracted as shown in below image. We can copy, move or delete the template from here.

Build Configuration Templates
Build configuration templates define settings that can be reused by different build configurations ⑦

+ Create template

Name		Build Steps		
gradleTemplate	Used in 1 configuration	Gradle	Edit	More ▾
		Copy template...		
		Move template...		

Subprojects
Subprojects can be used to group build configurations and defir   Delete template...

+ Create subproject   + Create subproject from URL

Deleting a template is not allowed if that template is referenced by any build configuration. To delete such templates, you need to detach it from any builds that are using it as shown in below image.

7. Build steps

7.1 Various build steps

Each build can have 1 or more build steps. Build steps are the actions that we want to perform as a part of the build process like installing packages, dependencies, compiling the project, executing the tests, publishing the artifacts etc.

Configuration of the build step depends upon the runner type of the step.

We can have below types of runners in TeamCity.

1. Nuget Installer
2. Test
3. Visual Studio Solution runner for compiling the source
4. Command line
5. MSTest
6. Gradle
7. IntelliJ IDEA project

New Build Step

Runner type:

New Build Step

Runner type:

-- Choose build runner type --

IntelliJ IDEA Project

Maven

MSBuild

MSpec

NAnt

NuGet Installer

NuGet Pack

NuGet Publish

NUnit

Powershell

Rake

Simple Build Tool (Scala)

Visual Studio (sln)

Visual Studio 2003

Visual Studio Tests

Xcode Project

7.2 Build steps for Gradle project

We have already seen all important settings of a typical build configurations. All settings in the build configurations are similar like general settings, VCS, triggers, failure conditions. What differs is the build steps. For different projects, we have to provide different build steps.

In this topic, we are going to look at build steps for a gradle project in TeamCity.

In build steps section, click on add a build step and select the gradle runner as shown in below image.

Gradle runners needs 2 very important settings.

1. build file - By default, it is **build.gradle** But you can change it as per your requirement.
2. task - any valid task name. You can find the list of commonly used tasks on gradle tasks article. Here we have mentioned **clean build** task.

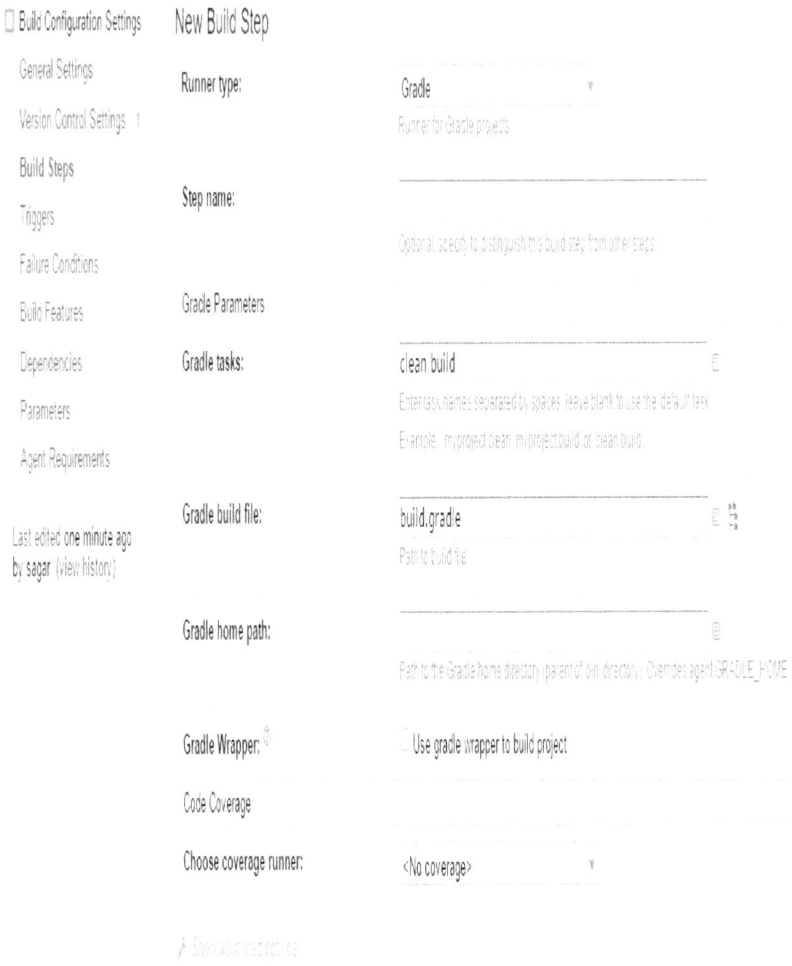

Build Configuration Settings

New Build Step

General Settings

Version Control Settings 1

Build Steps

Triggers

Failure Conditions

Build Features

Dependencies

Parameters

Agent Requirements

Last edited one minute ago
by sagar (view history)

Runner type:

Gradle

Runner for Gradle projects

Step name:

Optional, specify to distinguish this build step from other steps

Gradle Parameters

Gradle tasks:

clean build

Enter task names separated by spaces, leave blank to use the default task

Example: myproject:clean myproject:build or clean build

Gradle build file:

build.gradle

Path to build file

Gradle home path:

Path to the Gradle home directory (parent of bin directory). Overrides agent GRADLE_HOME

Gradle Wrapper:

Use gradle wrapper to build project

Code Coverage

Choose coverage runner:

<No coverage>

gradle clean build task in TeamCity

If you want to measure code coverage, you can use any of the available code coverage tool provided by IntelliJ IDEA or JaCoCo.

Below image shows the sample gradle build output.

gradle build log in TeamCity

7.3 Build steps for Maven project

In this topic, you will learn how to set up a build steps for maven project in TeamCity.

As shown in below image, you have to select runner type as Maven. Then you have to provide the goals to be executed. By default, it uses POM.xml in the root directory of the project. You may also run code coverage process along with test goal which gives report on how many classes were covered by tests.

Here is the list of some of the popular maven goals that can be used.

1. test - execute tests using surefire plugin. We can also pass various parameters to maven JUnit test goal and maven testNG test goal
2. verify - executes unit tests as well as does verification provided by plugins
3. install
4. site
5. deploy

TC | Projects   Changes   Agents 1 []   Build Queue 0

Administration > [] <Root project> > [] Maven Project > [] CompileMavenBuild

[] Build Configuration Settings

General Settings

Version Control Settings 1

Build Step: Maven

Triggers

Failure Conditions

Build Features

Dependencies

Parameters

Agent Requirements

Last edited moments ago
by sagar (view history)

Build Step

| Runner type: | Maven |
| | Runs Maven builds |

Step name:

Optional, specify to distinguish this build step from other steps

| Goals: | clean test-compile |
| | Space-separated goals to execute |

| Path to POM file: | pom.xml |

The specified path should be relative to the checkout directory

Code Coverage

Choose coverage runner: JaCoCo

Classfile directories or jars: Type classfile directories or jars

org.softproat.*

maven build step in TeamCity

Below image shows that sample build log.

maven build log in TeamCity

7.4 Build steps for .Net project

In this topic, we will learn how to add build steps for .Net project in TeamCity.

Some of the popular build steps for .Net project are given below.

1. .Net process runner
2. MSBuild
3. Visual Studio tests
4. Visual Studio project (.sln)

Below image shows how to configure MSBuild runner.

MSBuild runner in TeamCity

Below image shows how to configure Visual studio tests runner. There are 2 types of Test Engines available for running tests.

1. MSTest
2. VSTest

Visual Studio Tests runner in TeamCity

Below image shows the sample build log for above configuration.

.Net test build log in TeamCity

7.5 Build steps for command line

In this topic, let us learn how to write build step using command line in TeamCity.

Command line runner can be used to run Windows as well as Linux commands. If build is running on windows machine, cmd.exe is used to execute your command. If build is running on Linux machine, bash shell is used to execute command.

Below image shows how we have configured command line runner to execute windows command. Please note that instead of running a single command, you can also run windows batch file or shell script as well.

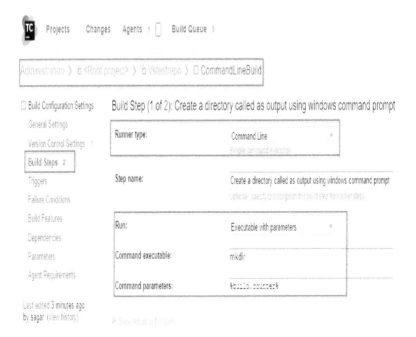

Below image shows the sample build log for above build configuration. Note that it is creating the directory with name 5 (Build counter).

7. 6 Powershell runner build step

In this topic, you will learn how to set up a Powershell build in TeamCity.

Please note that we can either provide the script content or the path of Powershell file to be executed as shown in below image.

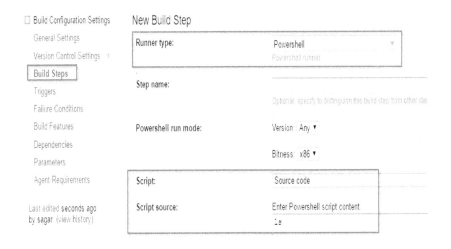

Powershell runner in TeamCity

Below image shows the sample build log of above build. It lists the files and directories in current directory.

Powershell build log in TeamCity

7.7 Duplicate code finder runner

TeamCity allows us to find the duplicate code in Java and .Net projects.

Below image shows how we can add a build step to find the duplicates in TeamCity.

Duplicate finder runner for Java in TeamCity

Similarly we can have a duplicate finder for .Net projects. Once we run this build, on overview tab of the build page, we can see the count of duplicates found as shown in below image.

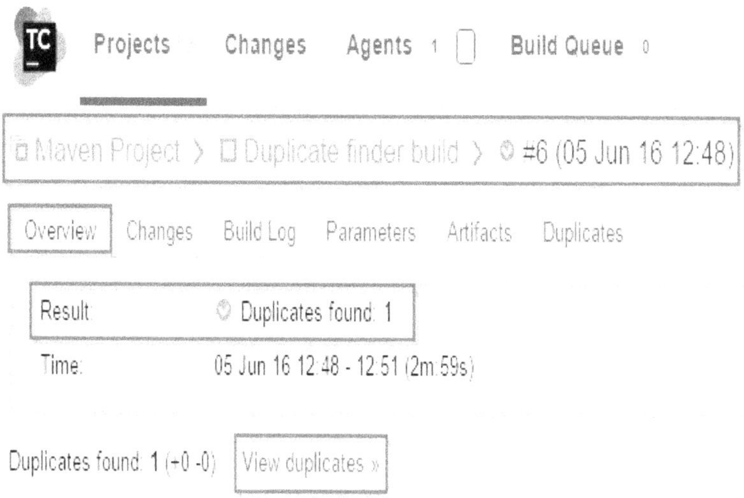

Duplicates tab shows the instances of duplicate as well as actual duplicate code and files as shown in below image.

Duplicates tab showing duplicate code in TeamCity

8. Build actions

8.1 Running builds

When we create the new build configuration in the project, it is displayed in the project overview tab.

You can do below tasks on project overview tab.

1. We can kick off build by clicking the run button next to it. The running build is marked with revolving green icon.
2. We can also view how long it will take to finish the build run.
3. We can stop the running build by clicking on the stop button next to it.
4. If there are multiple builds in the project, you can run only one build at a time with one build agent.
5. If you try to run other build, it is put into the end of build queue if there are not enough build agents available.But if you want to put the build on the top of the queue, you can do that by editing the build queue. In fact, you can re-order the builds in build queue as you like.

You can also run the customized builds as shown in below image. We can run build on priority and on specific agent with extra parameters.

Run customised build in TeamCity

8.2 Viewing the build run history and results

To view the build run history, you can click on build name in Project Overview tab. This will open build page.

The build page has below tabs.

1. Overview (Default tab) - pending changes, current status and recent history
2. History - shows entire history of the build runs
3. Change log - shows the build runs and changes made in the source files
4. Issue log -
5. Statistics - we can add various charts to see the build run data
6. Compatible agents - Shows the list of compatible build agents
7. Pending changes - Shows the changes that have not been included in any build run yet.
8. Settings - shows the settings of the build.
9. Web hooks

Viewing build history in TeamCity

Viewing build log and artifacts in TeamCity

8.3 Environment variables in TeamCity

Here is the list of useful environment variables in TeamCity.

1. TEAMCITY_BUILDCONF_NAME- stores the name of build configuration
2. TEAMCITY_GIT_PATH - path of git
3. TEAMCITY_JRE - JRE path being used
4. TEAMCITY_PROJECT_NAME - name of TeamCity project

5. COMPUTERNAME- Name of the computer running the build
6. BUILD_NUMBER - build number

You can access these variables in Java using below code. In other languages, you can use the language specific code to read environment variables.

```
Map<String, String> env = System.getenv();
        for (String envName : env.keySet())
{
            System.out.println(envName + "
--- > " + env.get(envName));
        }
```

8.4 Pinning builds

We can pin any build run as shown in below image. The main benefit of pinning the build is that build is not removed during cleanup process of TeamCity.

Pending changes   No pending changes

Current status   Idle

Recent history

Filter by tag   sleep   ✓ Show canceled and failed to start bu

Pinned build won't be removed from the history list until you unpin it.

#3	Tests passed 4	None	reply2sagar (1)	01 Jun 16 17:59	2m 48s	Sagar-Windows10	sleep	
#2	Tests passed 4	None	No changes	29 May 16 18:06	38s	Sagar-Windows10	None	
#1	Tests passed 4	None	No changes	29 May 16 16:41	4m 33s	Sagar-Windows10	None	

Pin build

result after adding the sleep

Tags:

sleep

[Pin]   Cancel

8.5 Build investigations

When builds fail, we need to investigate the reason of failure. TeamCity allows us to investigate any build. Below image shows how you can investigate a build.

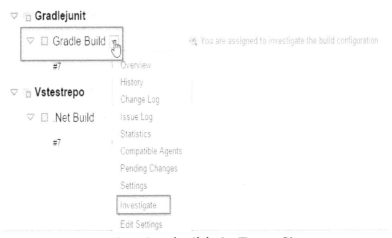

Investigating builds in TeamCity

In below pop up, you can assign the investigation to specific user and also add a comment.

Investigate build pop up in TeamCity

You can view builds under your investigation as shown in below image. Once the issue is resolved, you can mark the build as fixed.

Viewing builds under your investigation in TeamCity

8.6 Tagging builds

Tagging helps you to manage the important build runs very easily.

Below image shows how to tag specific build run in TeamCity.

tag build in TeamCity

Below image shows that we have added tag "review" to .Net build #4

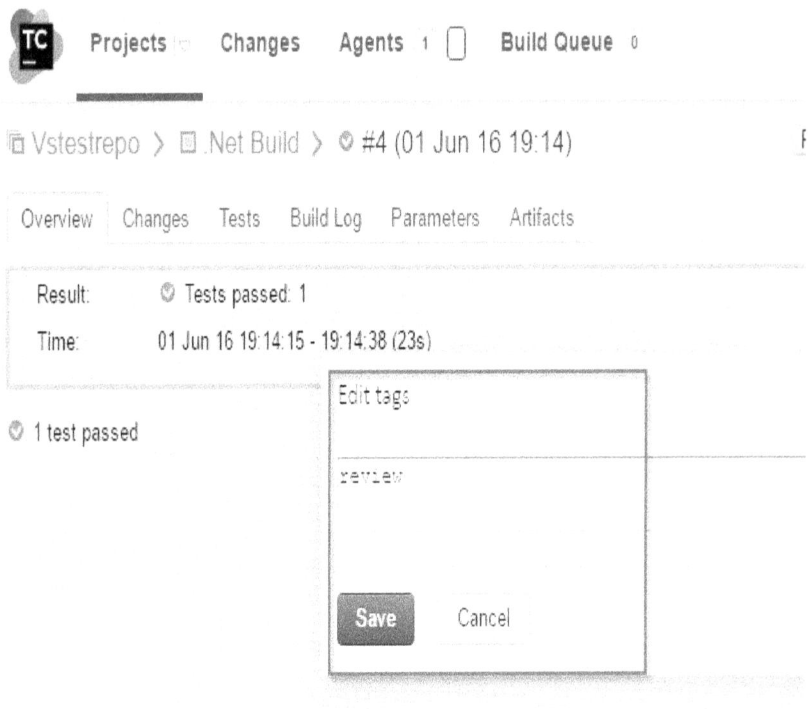

Tag build pop up in TeamCity

Below image shows that we can easily filter tagged builds in TeamCity.

filtering builds based on tag names in TeamCity

8.7 Configuring and Viewing artifacts of build

We can configure build in TeamCity in such a way that it stores output of the build on the server which we can access later on for troubleshooting purpose.

Below image shows how to instruct build to save certain files as an artifact. All files in directory /target/surefire-reports/** will be stored as an artifacts.

Artifact paths settings in TeamCity

Below image shows how to view artifacts generated by a typical build.

Viewing artifacts in TeamCity

9. Build agents in TeamCity

9.1 Setting up the build agents

TeamCity server supports multiple build agents. A build agent is an actual machine or virtual machine where the builds are run and tests are executed.

Each build agent should have supporting software required for building the project.

For example - If you want to build and test .net based project, you need to have .net compiler and MSTest to execute the tests on that build agent.

You can install the build agent from agents page.

9.2 Enable and disable build agent

To enable or disable the build agents, you have to go to agents page as shown in below image. Agents page (Connected tab) shows all connected agents. Below image shows that there is only one connected build agent.

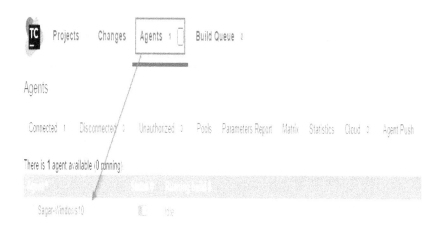

Build agents page in TeamCity

Then click on the build agent that you want to enable or disable. Below page shows the specific agent summary. Just click on Disable agent button to disable build agent. To enable the build agent, click on Enable agent button.

Disable Build agent in TeamCity

9.3 View build agent summary

To view build agent summary, you have to go to the Agents page as shown in below image.

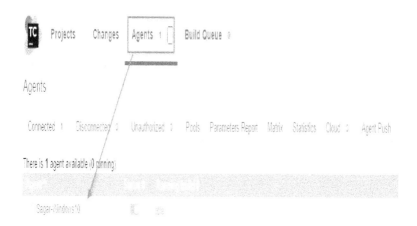

On agent page, click on the agent name for which you want to view summary. Below image shows the summary for build agent - activation.

Build summary shows below details.

1. If agent is connected or not
2. If agent is authorized or not
3. If agent is enabled or disabled. We can also enable/disable build agent.
4. IP address and port of build agent
5. Operating system of build agent
6. Name of the pool to which this build agent belongs

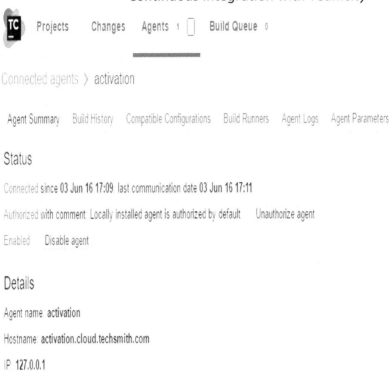

Build agent summary in TeamCity

9.4 View build history of an agent

To view build history of a build agent, open the build agent page as shown in below page and click on Build history tab.

Build history tab shows below details.

1. list of all build runs executed on selected build agent
2. It also shows when the build was run and if build was successful or failed.
3. You can click on the build configuration or build run result to view more details about them.

| TC | Projects | Changes | Agents 1 | | Build Queue 0 |

Connected agents > activation

Agent Summary | Build History | Compatible Configurations | Build Runners | Agent Logs | Agent Parameters

11 builds were run on this agent

Maven Project :: Maven tests Build	#3	✓ Tests passed: 1
Vstestrepo :: Net Build	#4	✓ Tests passed: 1
Vstestrepo :: Net Build	#3	⊘ MSTest execution failure (new)
Vstestrepo :: Net Build	#2	✓ Success
Vstestrepo :: Net Build	#1	✓ Success
Maven Project :: Maven tests Build	#2	✓ Tests passed: 1

View build history of an agent in TeamCity

9.5 Viewing build agent logs

We can view logs of any build agent as shown in below image.

Important types of logs that can be viewed are mentioned below.

1. launcher log
2. teamcity-agent log
3. build log
4. vcs log

Viewing build agent logs in TeamCity

9.6 Managing compatible configurations on a build agent

You can view the build configurations that are compatible with specific build agent from compatible configuration tab on a build agent page.

Below image shows that build configurations from 3 projects can be run on selected build agent. It also shows if there are any build configurations that can not be run on selected agent.

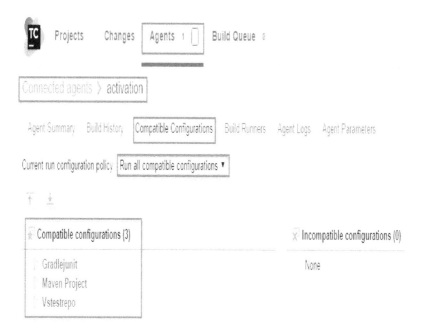

We can also assign specific build configurations to a build agent as shown in below image.

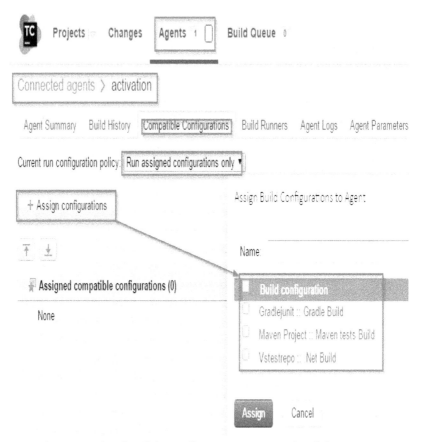

Assigning the build configurations to build agent in TeamCity

9.7 View build runners

Build runners are nothing but tools installed on build agent.

To view build runners of a specific agent, go to agent page and then click on build runners tab as shown in below image.

Some of the popular build runners are mentioned below.

1. Ant
2. Gradle
3. Maven
4. MSBuild
5. Visual Studio tests

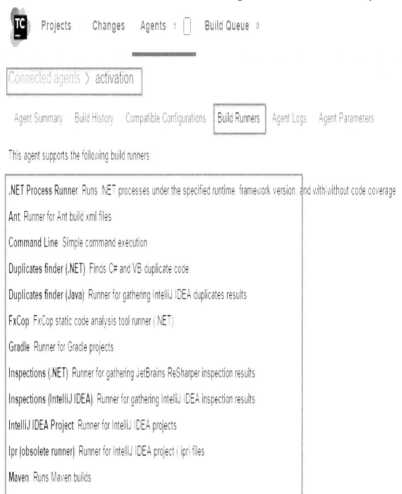

Viewing build runners of build agent in TeamCity

9.8 Viewing build agent parameters

We can view 3 types of parameters in TeamCity as shown in below image.

1. System properties
2. Environment variables
3. Configuration parameters

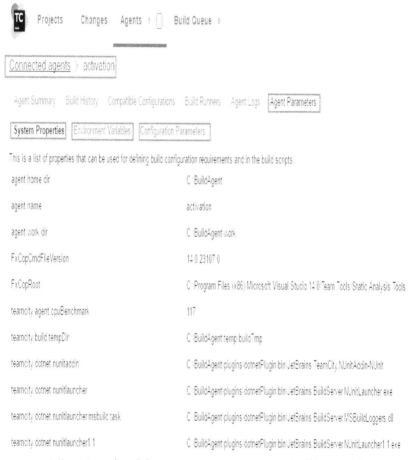

Viewing build agent parameters in TeamCity

9.9 Build agent pools

TeamCity server runs builds on multiple build agents at the same time. In big software projects, we often need to dedicate some build agents to execute specific builds. Or we have a requirement like build agents should be divided into 2 categories say those required for developers and those required for Testing guys.

To manage the build agents more efficiently, we can use agent pools. Agent pool is nothing but a group of build agent dedicated to certain category.

Create new build agent pool in TeamCity

119

As shown in below image, we can assign agents and projects to specific pool.

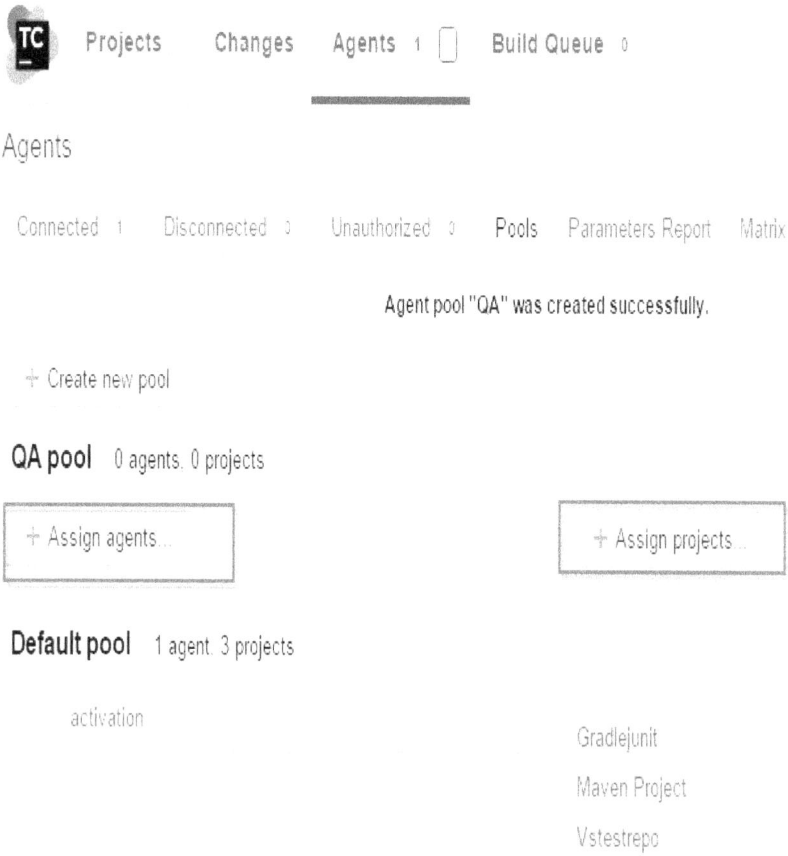

TC   Projects   Changes   Agents 1   [ ]   Build Queue 0

Agents

Connected 1   Disconnected 3   Unauthorized 3   Pools   Parameters Report   Matrix

Agent pool "QA" was created successfully.

+ Create new pool

QA pool   0 agents. 0 projects

+ Assign agents...   + Assign projects...

Default pool   1 agent. 3 projects

activation

Gradlejunit

Maven Project

Vstestrepo

assign agents and projects to pool in TeamCity

10. Tracking changes

In TeamCity, We can easily track changes made in the VCS by developers as shown in below image.

In below example, we have used git as a VCS. By default, TeamCity polls the git repository server (github/bitbucket etc) after every 1 minute. If TeamCity detects any new commits or changes, we can view those changes from Changes page.

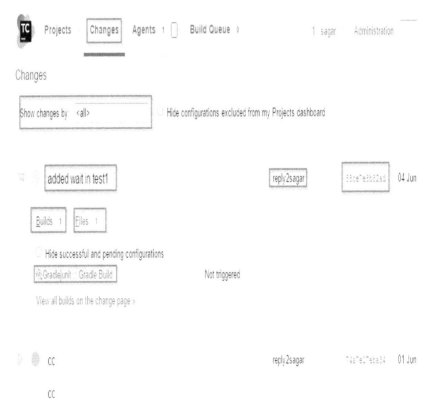

tracking changes in TeamCity

Ensure that you have selected show changes by all in the drop down. As you can see in above image, we can see below details on changes.

1. Commit id, author id and commit message
2. Builds impacted by the changes
3. Date when the changes were introduced

11. Managing Build Queue

We can have multiple build agents in TeamCity. So multiple builds can be run simultaneously on different agents. But sometimes, build agents are not enough to run the builds because at a time one agent runs only one build.

In this scenario, if you try to run extra build, that build is put in the build queue. Whenever the compatible agent is free, that build is assigned to that agent automatically. Below image shows how the build queue looks like in TeamCity.

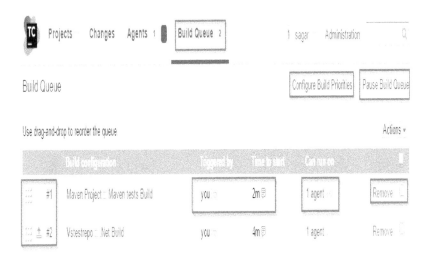

Build queue in TeamCity

Builds are picked from queue in ascending order to run. For example - in above image, build with id #1 will be run before build with id #2.

From build queue page, you can do below things.

1. View all builds that are in the queue and also view who triggered it and expected time to start
2. Configure build priorities
3. Pause and resume build queue
4. Remove specific build from the queue
5. It also shows the name of agent on which specific build can run
6. We can also reorder the position of the builds which helps us to run specific build early or delay it's execution

11.1 Configuraing build priorities in queue

We can configure the build queue priorities from Build Queue page.

By default, when we add a build to the build queue, that build is given priority as 0. But if want to prioritize any build, we can do so by assigning that build a higher priority.

Configuring build priorities in TeamCity

When you click on create new priority class, you are taken to below page.

Creating new priority class in TeamCity

adding build to priority class in TeamCity

As you can see in above images, we have added the Maven tests build to higher priority class (99 - priority). So next time, when maven tests build is added to the queue, it is always added at the front of the queue and executed before any other builds in the queue.

12. Personalizing TeamCity

12.1 Favorite builds

You can add any build to your favorites as shown in below image. Adding build to favorites helps you manage it very easily.

Adding build to favorites in TeamCity

To access the favorite builds, you can click on small arrow near your user name in TeamCity Dashboard.

Accessing favorite builds in TeamCity

12.2 Personal settings and tools in TeamCity

In TeamCity, you can make lot of personal settings as mentioned below.

1. Your name
2. Email address
3. VCS user names
4. Add notification rules for any builds

| TC | Projects | Changes | Agents | 1 | | Build Queue | 0 | | 1 | sagar | Admini |

My Favorite Builds

My Settings & Tools

My Investigations

My Settings & Tools

General   Groups   Notification Rules

Log out

General

Watched Builds and Notifications

Username   sagar   Edit

Email Notifier   Edit

Name

You are not watching any build configurations

Email address

IDE Notifier   Edit

You are not watching any build configurations

Current password

Jabber Notifier   Edit

New password

Jabber account

You are not watching any build configurations

Confirm new password.

Windows Tray Notifier   Edit

Settings and tools in TeamCity

129

13. More administration settings

13.1 Global settings in TeamCity

Global settings can be accessed from Administration page as shown in below image. These settings apply to all builds configured in the server. But you can override them in each build as well.

Here is the list of important settings.

1. Server URL - You change the server url using this setting
2. Maximum build artifact size - This is used to define the maximum size of the artifact created by any build. Any artifacts larger than this size will be deleted automatically.
3. Build execution timeout - Default build timeout is 0 which means that there is no restriction on how long the build runs. But if you want any build to finish execution withing specific duration of time, you can specify that time duration here.
4. Version control settings - Version control settings allow you to specify interval after which VCS should be polled for changes. If changes are detected, build will be triggered. But before adding build into queue, TeamCity waits for the specific duration called as quiet period. If more changes are

detected during quiet period, VCS changes check interval starts all over again.

Server Health	Data directory:	C:\Users\Sagar\BuildServer Browse
Audit		
	Artifact directories:	system\artifacts
User Management		New-line delimited paths to artifact directories used by the server. Artifac
Users		the first directory in the list. Relative paths are relative to TeamCity data
Groups		
	Caches directory:	C:\Users\Sagar\BuildServer\system\caches
Integrations		
NuGet	Server URL:	http://localhost:8888
Tools	Builds Settings	
Server Administration	Maximum build artifact file size:	300000000
Global Settings		in bytes. KB, MB, GB or TB suffixes are allowed. -1 indicates no limit
Authentication		
Email Notifier	Default build execution timeout:	0 minutes
Jabber Notifier		0 and negative values indicate no execution timeout
Agent Cloud	Version Control Settings	
Diagnostics	Default VCS changes check interval:	60 seconds
Backup		
Projects Import	Default VCS trigger quiet period:	60 seconds
Licenses		

global settings in TeamCity

13.2 NuGet integration in TeamCity

NuGet is the package manager for .Net projects. NuGet integration can be done from administration page as shown in below image.

Click on Enable NuGet server button.

Once NuGet server is enabled, you can provide the feed url to it.

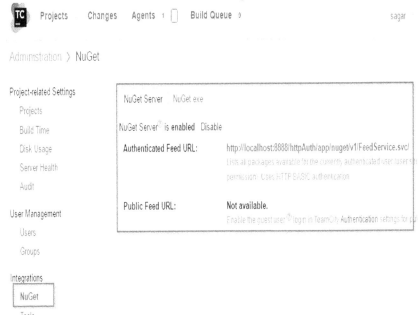

You can also install NuGet.exe from within TeamCity as shown in below image.

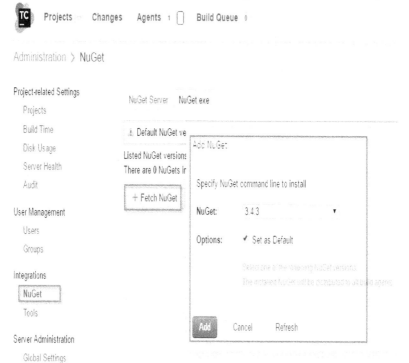

13.3 Viewing build time in TeamCity

You can view build time for all builds and projects in TeamCity from administration page as shown in below image.

We can do below things on Build time page.

1. View build time for all builds run in specific duration of time like yesterday, last week or last month.
2. We can view duration of builds from archived projects as well.
3. We can also sort the builds based upon build duration time. Thus we can find out fast and slow builds.

View build time for all builds and projects in TeamCity

13.4 Viewing build disk usage in TeamCity

You can view disk usage for all builds and projects in TeamCity from administration page as shown in below image.

We can do below things on Disk usage page.

1. View free disk space on TeamCity server
2. View disk usage for all builds
3. We can view disk usage of builds from archived projects as well.
4. We can also sort the builds based upon disk usage. Thus we can find out the builds consuming high/low disk space.

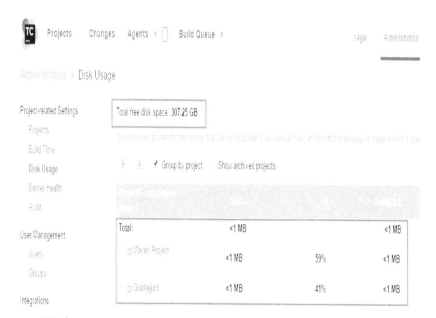

Disk usage per project and build in TeamCity

13.5 Audit and Actions in TeamCity

We can view audit and activities in TeamCity from administration page as shown in below image.

From Audit page, we can do below things.

1. View actions done by each user on each date.
2. We can filter the actions based on project name or build name.
3. We can also filter the actions done by specific user.
4. We can also view specific actions only like adding build to queue, pausing build, stopping build etc.

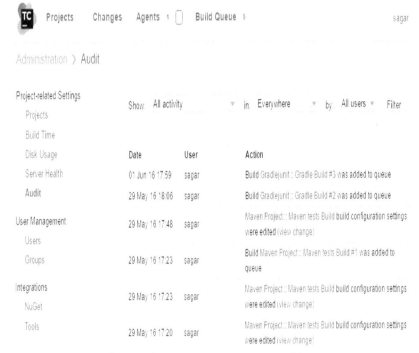

Audit and activities in TeamCity

13.6 Authentication settings in TeamCity

We can manage authentication settings of the TeamCity server from administration page as shown in below image.

authentication in TeamCity

13.7 Email server set up in TeamCity

You can configure email server settings in TeamCity so that you get any notifications of build failures on your email address.

Below image shows how you can set up email server in TeamCity through Administration page.

You need to provide below details to set up email server.

1. SMTP host name
2. SMTP port
3. SMTP login and password

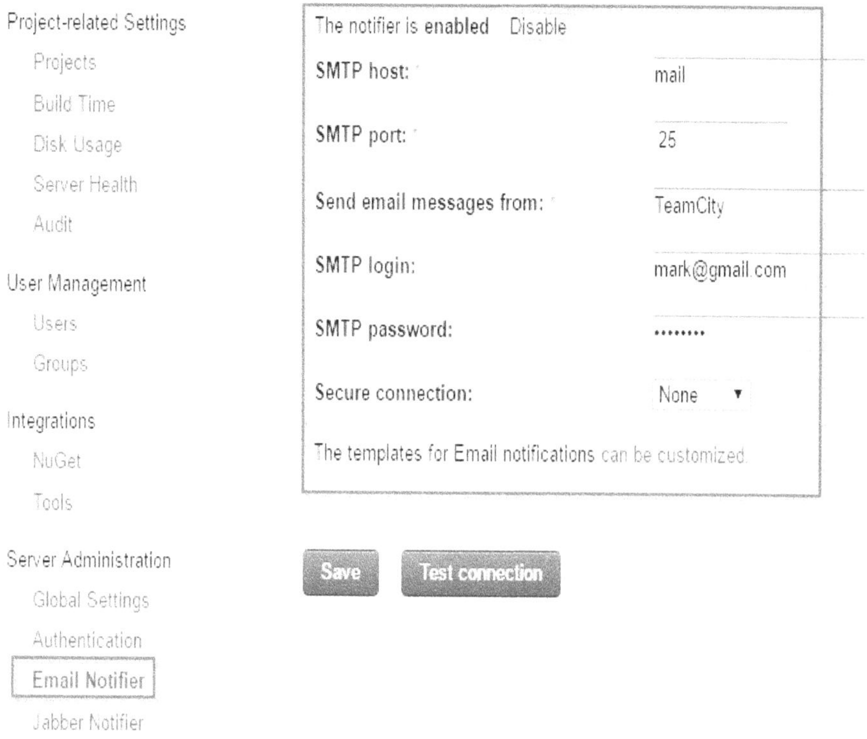

Project-related Settings
  Projects
  Build Time
  Disk Usage
  Server Health
  Audit

User Management
  Users
  Groups

Integrations
  NuGet
  Tools

Server Administration
  Global Settings
  Authentication
  Email Notifier
  Jabber Notifier

The notifier is enabled   Disable

SMTP host:	mail
SMTP port:	25
Send email messages from:	TeamCity
SMTP login:	mark@gmail.com
SMTP password:	••••••••
Secure connection:	None ▼

The templates for Email notifications can be customized.

Save   **Test connection**

Email server set up in TeamCity

13.8 Back up builds and projects in TeamCity

Sometimes, you need to backup builds and projects to clean up the server or to move the projects and builds to different TeamCity server.

To back up, you need to follow steps as shown in below image. You can provide the name of back up file and also specify the scope of backup. If you select Basic scope, items shown in below image are backed up. If you select custom, you can select what items you want to export from below list.

1. database
2. server settings, projects and builds configurations, plugins
3. settings history, triggers states etc
4. build logs
5. personal builds changes

Back up in TeamCity

13.9 Importing backup in TeamCity

You can import the build and project configuration settings from a back up file. If you do not how to take a back up of your server, please have a look at an article on how to back up TeamCity

Then go to the installation directory of new TeamCity server and put the backed up file at **{Home_Directory}\.BuildServer\import** then open the **Administration -> Projects Import** page of new TeamCity server. All project and build settings will be applied automatically. If TeamCity server does not find the back up file, it will give information message saying There are no backup files.

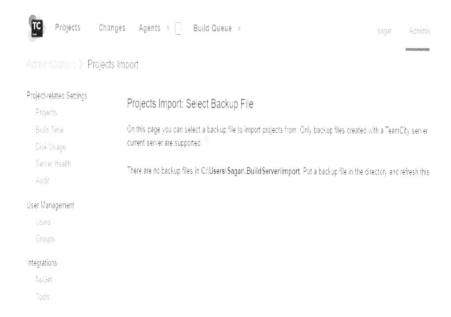

importing projects in TeamCity

13.10 Viewing license information

Below image shows how to view license information in TeamCity from Administration -> Licenses page.

Licenses page shows 3 important things about TeamCity.

1. TeamCity version and mode
2. Maximum number of authorized build agents
3. Maximum number of build configurations

License information in TeamCity

13.11 Cleaning up TeamCity server

You can clean up TeamCity server in 2 ways.

1. Manually
2. Periodically at scheduled time

To clean up TeamCity server, you have to go to clean up settings page as shown in below image. You can enable or disable the periodical clean up and also mention the time at which clean up should start. It also shows previous clean ups.

To manually clean up, you can click on Start clean up now button.

Cleaning up TeamCity server

13.12 Usage statistics in TeamCity

You can view Usage statistics in TeamCity by navigating to Administration -> Usage Statistics page.

This page shows very useful information as mentioned below.

1. General - count of agents, builds, projects, users etc
2. Server load
3. VCS types
4. Build runners like maven, gradle, MSBuild, Visual Studio tests
5. Server configuration

TC_   Projects   Changes   Agents 1 ☐   Build Queue 0   sagar   Administration

Administration > Usage Statistics

Project-related Settings

Projects

Build Time

Disk Usage

Server Health

Audit

User Management

Users

Groups

Integrations

NuGet

Tools

Server Administration

Global Settings

Authentication

Email Notifier

Jabber Notifier

Please let us learn a bit more about your TeamCity usage. We are not watching you and not collecting any user- or project-sen numbers. Help us improve the tool!

✓ Periodically send this statistics to JetBrains

Usage statistics data was collected 56 minutes ago.   Collect Now

General

Connected agents (all)	1
Connected agents (authorized only)	1 (100%)
Connected agents (unidirectional connection)	0 (0%)
Agent pools	1
Build configurations	2
Active build configurations	2 (100%)
Active build configurations with several VCS roots	0 (0%)
Snapshot dependencies	0
Artifact dependencies	0
Projects	3
Archived projects	0 (0%)
User groups	1

Maven Usages

mavenSelection default

Server Configuration

Server ID	20c272f0-48fc-49bc-8f3
Platform	Windows 10 10.0 amd6
Login modules	Built-in
HTTP authentication schemes	Basic HTTP
Database version	HSQL Database Engine
JDBC driver version	HSQL Database Engine
Java version	1.8.0_77

Usage statistics in TeamCity

13.13 Plugins in TeamCity

You can view, upload and browse plugins in TeamCity by navigating to Administration -> Plugins List.

As shown in below page, there are 84 plugins installed on current TeamCity server.

Plugins in TeamCity

www.ingramcontent.com/pod-product-compliance
Lightning Source LLC
Chambersburg PA
CBHW052146070326
40689CB00050B/2259